Written by: Calandra Tucker

Manufactured in the United States

Illustrations by Cameron Wilson for Soulsimplicity Design and Publishing.
For illustration inquires visit camdaillastrata.com.

SPECIAL THANKS:

First and foremost, I give thanks to my Heavenly Father for guiding and inspiring me to complete this book. I am truly grateful for His grace and blessings throughout this journey.

To my family, your unwavering support and encouragement mean the world to me. I love you all more than words can express!

A heartfelt thank you to Cameron Wilson—your dedication and talent have been instrumental in bringing my vision to life. I couldn't have done it without you!

I AM WHO I AM: JUST LET ME BE

BY CALANDRA TUCKER

ILLUSTRATED BY CAMERON WILSON

Mom and Dad, I am who God made me to be.
I can't be Nicholas, Jackie, or even Bobby.

We may have the same DNA and even look alike in some ways,
but that's all where it stops because we are different and that's where is stays.

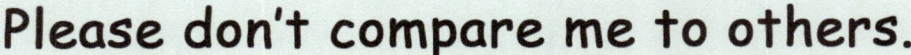

Please don't compare me to others.

I can only be me, not dad,
my siblings, or even mother.

I have a great personality, character, and am really good at many things.

Please give me the chance to show you just how great of a gift my life brings!

I love being me just the way that I am.
God made only one me, so please
accept that I am who I am!

Now that you are open to allowing me to be me, look at all the great things I can be.

I can be a doctor.

I can be a mechanic.

I can be a teacher.

I can be a preacher.

Or even a news anchor on TV.

When you give me the freedom to explore just who I can be, it makes my heart glad that you see what I see.

I have all the potential in the world to be someone great. Your guidance and encouragement are just what I need to push me along at any rate.

I will learn all I can, try until I succeed, help others along the way, because that is what you've instilled in me.

I am destined for great and magnificent things and I'm extremely excited to show you who I will be!

Mom and dad thank you for listening, hearing, and allowing me to be the original God created when He made me. I love you!

I
LOVE
BEING
ME!

NOW IT'S YOUR TURN!

Every person in your family is wonderfully unique, just like you've seen in this story. Now, let's take some time to celebrate the special qualities that make you and your family amazing!

What makes you feel proud to be yourself?

What do you think is the most unique thing about your family?

How can you and your family show more love and encouragement to one another?

DREAM BIG!

What do you want to be? What are your biggest dreams?

For Child: This is your special space to dream BIG! Draw or write your goals here, no matter how small or how big they might seem. Remember, anything is possible when you believe in yourself!

A Note From Your Biggest Fan:
Loved ones, leave a special note of encouragement below to remind your child how much you believe in their amazing potential.

FUTURE MEMORIES

Families write or draw something fun you'd like to do together in the future.

HEARTFELT MESSAGES

Write or draw a small note of encouragement for each family member and share it with them.

Thank you for taking the time to read I Am Who I Am: Just Let Me Be. It means so much that you've chosen to share this journey of love, acceptance, and individuality with your family.

I hope this book has sparked meaningful conversations and reminded you of the incredible gift each person brings simply by being themselves. Your support inspires me to continue creating stories that touch hearts and bring families closer together.

Remember, the greatest gift we can give one another is love and the freedom to be exactly who we are.

With heartfelt appreciation,

Calandra Tucker